1 Corinthians

A Basic Bible Study

David Young

CONTENTS

Introduction

Author and Background

The apostle Paul founded the Church at Corinth during his second missionary journey that lasted from 49 to 54 AD (Acts 15:36–18:22). Paul stayed in Corinth for a year and a half (Acts 18:11). After departing Corinth, and while on his 3rd missionary journey, Paul received word that there were problems in the church at Corinth (1 Cor. 1), and he wrote the first letter to give advice on how to handle these problems.

> **1ˢᵗ Missionary Journey (47 - 48 A.D.)**
> No books were written
> **2nd Missionary Journey (49 - 54 A.D.)**
> 1 Thessalonians (51 - 52 A.D.) Written from Corinth
> 2 Thessalonians (51 - 52 A.D.) Written from Corinth
> **3rd Missionary Journey (54 - 58 A.D.)**
> ➢ 1 Corinthians (54 A.D.) Written from Ephesus
> Galatians (54 A.D.) Written from Greece
> 2 Corinthians (57 A.D.) Written from Macedonia
> Romans (57 A.D.) Written from Corinth
> **First Roman Imprisonment (61 - 63 A.D.)**
> Ephesians (62 A.D.) Written from Rome
> Philippians (62 A.D.) Written from Rome
> Colossians (A.D.) Written from Rome
> Philemon (62 A.D.) Written from Rome
> **Between First & Second Imprisonments (63 - 66 A.D.)**
> 1 Timothy (63 A.D.) Written from Macedonia
> Titus (66 A.D.) Written from Ephesus
> **Second Roman Imprisonment (67 A.D.)**
> 2 Timothy (67 A.D.) Written from Rome

The above dates are approximate. Various commentaries and Bible handbooks will have different dates.

The city of Corinth was a very large and prosperous seaport and a key city in the Roman Empire. In 146 B.C. Corinth rebelled against

Introduction

Rome, and the Roman army destroyed the city. Nearly one hundred years later, Julius Caesar rebuilt the city as a Roman colony, and most of the early settlers were of the working class or Freedmen. Freedmen were former soldiers or public servants who were granted land as part of their retirement. A smaller number were wealthy merchants and businessmen. The city gained a reputation for immoral behavior. Plato used the term "Corinthian girl" to refer to a prostitute (Life Application Commentary, p. 4).

Paul's Letters

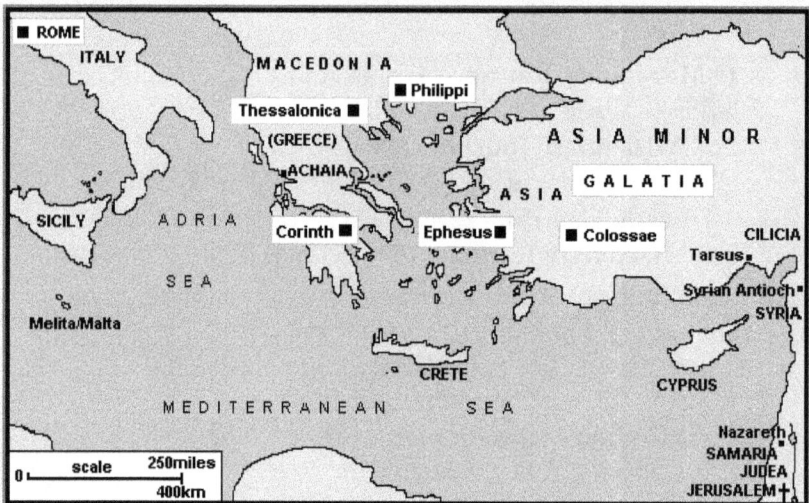

1 Corinthians Chapter 1

1 Corinthians 1:1-9 Introduction

Paul, called to be an apostle of Jesus Christ through the will of God, and our brother Sosthenes, ² to the church of God which is at Corinth—those who are sanctified in Christ Jesus, called saints, with all who call on the name of our Lord Jesus Christ in every place, both theirs and ours: ³ Grace to you and peace from God our Father and the Lord Jesus Christ.

⁴ I always thank my God concerning you for the grace of God which was given you in Christ Jesus, ⁵ that in everything you were enriched in him, in all speech and all knowledge— ⁶ even as the testimony of Christ was confirmed in you— ⁷ so that you come behind in no gift, waiting for the revelation of our Lord Jesus Christ, ⁸ who will also confirm you until the end, blameless in the day of our Lord Jesus Christ. ⁹ God is faithful, through whom you were called into the fellowship of his Son, Jesus Christ our Lord.

1:1. Paul begins nearly all of his letters to churches by declaring that he is an apostle appointed by the will of God. There were some in Corinth who denied that Paul was an apostle (1 Cor. 9:1-3; 2 Cor. 11:12-15). Sosthenes was the leader of the Jewish Synagogue when Paul visited the city on his second missionary journey (Acts 18:17), and Paul baptized him (1 Cor. 1:16).

1:2. The letter is addressed to

- The church of God which is at Corinth
- Those who are sanctified
- Called to be saints

The words sanctified and saints come from the same Greek word *hagios* (hag-e-os), which can mean holy, sanctified, or saints. It can also mean to be set apart for divine purposes. In the Old Testament, the Hebrew equivalent was applied to the furnishings in the tabernacles, the altar, and the instruments used to handle sacrifices at the altar.

From God's perspective, all Christians are saints (set-apart) even when they do not behave like saints. Later in this letter, Paul accuses the people of not being spiritual but rather carnal (1 Cor. 3:1-3). They were saints, but some of them were behaving in un-Christian ways.

Questions:

Are you comfortable with the terms sanctified and saint?

Is this how you see yourself?

1:4-7. Paul reminds the people of how much they are blessed. They have received the grace of God, they are rich in speech and knowledge, and they have spiritual gifts (they are at the forefront of churches in this regard).

1:7-9. To be sure, God will confirm and preserve them until his return (the Second coming of Christ).

Paul is very wise. He begins the letter with words of grace and affirmation before confronting them with the issues he wants to address.

Questions:

From what we see so far, what is Paul's opinion of the church at Corinth?

Is Paul writing to criticize this church or to strengthen them?

1 Corinthians 1:10-17   Divisions in the Church

[10] Now I beg you, brothers, through the name of our Lord, Jesus Christ, that you all speak the same thing, and that there be no divisions among you, but that you be perfected together in the same mind and in the same judgment. [11] For it has been reported to me concerning you, my brothers, by those who are from Chloe's household, that there are contentions among you. [12] Now I mean this, that each one of you says, "I follow Paul," "I follow Apollos," "I follow Cephas," and "I follow Christ." [13] Is Christ divided? Was Paul crucified for you? Or were you baptized into the name of Paul? [14] I thank God that I baptized none of you except Crispus and Gaius, [15] so that no one should say that I had baptized you into my own name. [16] (I also baptized the household of Stephanas; besides them, I do not know whether I baptized any other.) [17] For Christ sent me not to baptize, but to preach the gospel—not in wisdom of words, so that the cross of Christ would not be made void.

1:10-13. Paul pleads for unity in the church. Chloe was probably a wealthy businesswoman, and members of her household traveled on business. They reported to Paul that there were divisions in the church. Different ones said, "I follow Paul," "I follow Apollos," "I follow Cephas," and "I follow Christ."

The church at Corinth was a typical big-city church. It included a diverse mixture of Greeks and Jews, and a few were wealthy, but most were working class. Most likely, those of Jewish background were drawn to Peter while the Greeks were drawn to Paul. Apollos was a very polished speaker and would have been appealing to the upper-class Greeks.

This is almost like denominations! I'm Baptist, I'm Methodist, I'm Lutheran.

Question: Is it possible to have absolute unity in the church? Why do we have denominations?

1:14-17   Baptism vs the Cross

It is interesting that Paul says he was not sent to baptize (v. 17). He is
not saying that he did not baptize at all, but he is saying that baptizing
was not his primary calling. As an apostle, his primary calling was to
establish churches by preaching the gospel. In verse 16, he names
some of the people he did baptize, but this list is just those in
Corinth. Paul also baptized people in Philippi (Acts 16:25-34).

Paul is saying, you belong to Christ and his church, not to me or to
any other individual.

1 Corinthians 1:18-25   The Message of the Cross is Power

[18] For the message of the cross is foolishness to those who are
dying, but to us who are being saved it is the power of God. [19] For
it is written,

> "I will destroy the wisdom of the wise.
>   I will bring the discernment of the discerning to nothing."

[20] Where is the wise? Where is the scribe? Where is the debater of
this age? Has not God made foolish the wisdom of this
world? [21] For seeing that in the wisdom of God, the world through
its wisdom did not know God, it was God's good pleasure through
the foolishness of the preaching to save those who believe. [22] For
Jews ask for signs, Greeks seek after wisdom, [23] but we preach
Christ crucified, a stumbling block to Jews and foolishness to
Greeks, [24] but to those who are called, both Jews and Greeks,
Christ is the power of God and the wisdom of God; [25] because the
foolishness of God is wiser than men, and the weakness of God is
stronger than men.

1:20-23. Jews seek after signs. They seek to validate their religious
beliefs by supernatural signs. Greeks, on the other hand, prioritize
wisdom. They follow the Greek philosophers such as Socrates, Plato,
and Aristotle. Christ crucified on a cross is a problem for the Jews

because the Messiah was expected to be a mighty warrior who would defeat the Romans. How could this man who died like a criminal on a cross be the Messiah? He was also a problem for the Greeks because they did not expect any god to be in a human form and die a human death.

But to those to whom the Holy Spirit has opened their eyes,

(Vs 18) For the message of the cross is... the power of God.

(vs 24) Christ is the power of God and the wisdom of God.

(Rom. 1:16) For I am not ashamed of the gospel, because it is the power of God that brings salvation.

1:25. "Because the foolishness of God is wiser than men, and the weakness of God is stronger than men."

The foolishness of God... God's least amount of wisdom...is wiser than human wisdom. The weakness of God... God's least amount of strength... is stronger than human strength.

Questions:

Why is the message about the cross so important?

Why did God choose to save us through the death of Christ? Why can we not find salvation through human wisdom?

"If you declare with your mouth, 'Jesus is Lord,' and believe in your heart that God raised him from the dead, you will be saved. For it is with your heart that you believe and are justified, and it is with your mouth that you profess your faith and are saved". Rom. 10:9-10 NIV

Are we sometimes tempted to "dress the gospel up" in the language of the world to make it more attractive? What happens when we do that? What is meant by the term "user-friendly church?"

1 Corinthians 1:26-31   The Message of the Cross is Power (Part 2)

[26] For you see your brothers, that not many of you were wise according to the flesh, not many mighty, and not many noble when you were called; [27] but God chose the foolish things of the world that he might put to shame those who are wise. God chose the weak things of the world that he might put to shame the things that are strong. [28] God chose the lowly things of the world, and the things that are despised, and the things that do not exist, that he might bring to nothing the things that exist, [29] that no flesh should boast before God. [30] Because of him, you are in Christ Jesus, who was made to us wisdom from God, and righteousness and sanctification, and redemption, [31] that, as it is written, "He who boasts, let him boast in the Lord."

1:26-27. The majority of the people in Corinth were working-class people, and Paul reminds them of their backgrounds. God has chosen the common things, including common people, to bring forth the gospel.

1:26-28. "God chose the lowly things of the world, and the things that are despised, and the things that do not exist, that he might bring to nothing the things that exist."

God wants us to believe in Him through faith, not to trust in human wisdom, strength, or our own philosophies.

Questions:

The Hebrew concept of messiah was a strong, powerful warrior-king who would lead the people into battle. This kind of messiah would appeal to strong, powerful people.

Why does God speak and act through humble and weak things more than through human strength and wisdom? Why does God require faith, rather than show us his power all the time?

1 Corinthians Chapter 2

1 Corinthians 2:1-8   Human Wisdom Versus God's Power

[1] When I came to you, brothers, I did not come with excellence of speech or of wisdom, proclaiming to you the testimony of God. [2] For I determined not to know anything among you except Jesus Christ and him crucified. [3] I was with you in weakness, in fear, and in much trembling. [4] My speech and my preaching were not in persuasive words of human wisdom, but in demonstration of the Spirit and of power, [5] that your faith would not stand in the wisdom of men, but in the power of God.

[6] We speak wisdom, however, among those who are fully grown, yet a wisdom not of this world nor of the rulers of this world who are coming to nothing. [7] But we speak God's wisdom in a mystery, the wisdom that has been hidden, which God foreordained before the worlds for our glory, [8] which none of the rulers of this world has known. For had they known it, they would not have crucified the Lord of glory.

2:1. Paul continues his teaching that the gospel is not based on human wisdom; it is based on the power of God that comes through the cross of Christ. Paul did not attempt to win them to Christ through human arguments or Greek rhetoric, but only through the power of preaching the cross.

2:2. For I determined not to know anything among you except Jesus Christ and him crucified.

2:3. Why was Paul afraid? Perhaps he was afraid that his preaching would not be effective. Maybe the people would not accept the gospel of a crucified Christ.

Questions:

What does Paul mean in verse 4, about "the demonstration of the

Spirit and of power"? God used Paul to perform extraordinary miracles in Ephesus (Acts 19), but there is no record of him doing miracles in Corinth. Is powerful preaching just as miraculous as other types of miracles? How does powerful preaching draw men and women to Christ?

2:6 & 8. Some people think the "rulers of this world" refers to human rulers, and some think it refers to the demon forces that influence rulers (Eph. 6:12). What do you think it means?

1 Corinthians 2:9-16   The Mysteries of God's Word

⁹ But as it is written,

> "Things which no eye has seen, and no ear has heard,
>   which no human mind has understood,
>   the things God has prepared for those who love him."

¹⁰ But to us, God revealed them through the Spirit. For the Spirit searches all things, yes, the deep things of God. ¹¹ For who among men knows the things of a man except the spirit of the man which is in him? Even so, no one knows the things of God except God's Spirit. ¹² But we received not the spirit of the world, but the Spirit which is from God, that we might know the things that were freely given to us by God. ¹³ We also speak these things, not in words which man's wisdom teaches, but which the Holy Spirit teaches, comparing spiritual things with spiritual things. ¹⁴ Now the natural man does not receive the things of God's Spirit, for they are foolishness to him; and he cannot know them, because they are spiritually discerned. ¹⁵ But he who is spiritual discerns all things, and he himself is to be judged by no one. ¹⁶ "For who has known the mind of the Lord that he should instruct him?" But we have the mind of Christ.

2:10-15. God's plan and his word are mysteries; he reveals his mysteries to his people. We have received the Spirit of God (v. 12), and his Spirit teaches us the great mysteries of God (v. 13-15).

2:16. We have the mind of Christ. We must read this in the context of what Paul is saying. The wisdom of God is a mystery (v. 6-7). No one knows the thoughts of God except God himself (v. 11). The wisdom of God cannot be known through human wisdom, but as taught by the Holy Spirit (v. 13). Since we have the Holy Spirit, we are taught by the Spirit (vs. 10-12).

All Christians have the Holy Spirit, and therefore, we have the mind of Christ within us. The task for us is to surrender to Christ so that his mind can flow into our minds.

Questions:

2:16. What does it mean that we have the mind of Christ? What can we do to improve our understanding of God?

1 Corinthians Chapter 3

1 Corinthians 3:1-9   Revisiting the Divisions

[1] Brothers, I could not speak to you as to spiritual, but as to fleshly, as to babies in Christ. [2] I fed you with milk, not with solid food, for you were not yet ready. Indeed, you still are not ready, [3] for you are still fleshly. For insofar as there is jealousy, strife, and factions among you, are you not fleshly, and do you not walk in the ways of men? [4] For when one says, "I follow Paul," and another, "I follow Apollos," are you not fleshly?

[5] Who then is Apollos, and who is Paul, but servants through whom you believed, and each as the Lord gave to him? [6] I planted. Apollos watered. But God gave the increase. [7] So then neither he who plants is anything, nor he who waters, but God who gives the increase. [8] Now he who plants and he who waters are the same, but each will receive his own reward according to his own labor. [9] For we are God's fellow workers. You are God's field, God's building.

3:1-4. In chapter 1, Paul points out the divisions in the church. In chapter 2, he assures them that Greek philosophy and human wisdom are thot the means of knowing God. Now, in chapter 3, he points out that these divisions are indicators of spiritual immaturity. Paul opened the letter (1:23) by calling them "saints of God," but now he says they are babies in Christ and fleshly.

Question:

Can someone be a saint and still be spiritually immature at the same time?

What does it mean to be fleshly?

Unspiritual (J.B. Phillips)
Ordinary people (NASB)
People of the world (NLT)

3:5-7. Referring back to chapter 1, where Paul chastised them for being divided: Some of you say, "I follow Paul," "I follow Apollos," "I follow Cephas," and "I follow Christ." Paul now says, "Please understand that Apollos and I are just co-workers in God's field. I plant, Apollos waters what I have planted, but only God can make the fruit (converts) grow spiritually."

3:8. Each will receive his own reward according to his own labor. Paul and Apollos are not in competition with each other. Each person will be rewarded according to how faithful they are to their own calling and the talents and gifts given to them by the Spirit.

1 Corinthians 3:10-15   God's Workers

[10] According to the grace of God which was given to me, as a wise master builder, I laid a foundation, and another builds on it. But let each man be careful how he builds on it. [11] For no one can lay any other foundation than that which has been laid, which is Jesus Christ. [12] But if anyone builds on the foundation with gold, silver, costly stones, wood, hay, or straw, [13] each man's work will be revealed. For the Day will declare it, because it is revealed in fire; and the fire itself will test what sort of work each man's work is. [14] If any man's work remains which he built on it, he will receive a reward. [15] If any man's work is burned, he will suffer loss, but he himself will be saved, but as through fire.

3:10-13. When we work for God, some of the work comes from a pure heart with pure motives. But sometimes, we may do good works out of pride or guilt. Sometimes we may look down our noses at the very people we are serving. Good works from a heart of love are like gold and precious stones—they only get better when examined by fire. Works from an impure heart are destroyed when examined by fire.

3:14. Examination by fire is symbolic but may reflect the judgment of 2 Cor. 5:10. There are rewards in heaven, but no punishment. Heaven will be a highly organized place, with some people in positions of leadership or in positions where we can serve and honor God with greater effectiveness.

1 Corinthians 3:16-23   You are God's Temple

[16] Do you not know that you are God's temple and that God's Spirit lives in you? [17] If anyone destroys God's temple, God will destroy him; for God's temple is sacred, and you are that temple.

[18] Let no one deceive himself. If anyone thinks that he is wise among you in this world, let him become a fool that he may become wise. [19] For the wisdom of this world is foolishness with God. For it is written, "He has taken the wise in their craftiness." [20] And again, "The Lord knows the reasoning of the wise, that it is worthless." [21] Therefore, let no one boast in men. For all things are yours, [22] whether Paul, or Apollos, or Cephas, or the world, or life, or death, or things present, or things to come. All are yours, [23] and you are Christ's, and Christ is God's.

3:16-17. Verse 17 concludes with "and you are that temple." The NIV translates it "and you together are that temple." Paul is referring to the church as the collective body of Christians. Paul also refers to the church as the temple of God in Eph . 2:21 and 2 Cor. 6:16.

When Paul refers to destroying the temple of God, he may be referring to the divisions that are weakening the church. Since the church is made up of individuals, and the individuals together make up the church, what is true of one is true of the group. The Spirit lives in us individually and also in us as a group.

3:18-23. Paul returns again to the subject of wisdom. "For the wisdom of this world is foolishness with God" (v. 19).

Questions:

Why is Paul concerned that divisions and reliance on human wisdom might destroy the church?

3:17 God wants to protect the church. So much so that he threatens to "destroy" those who destroy the church; does this mean actual destruction, or perhaps severing them from the church? We will discuss this more in chapter 5 (1 Cor. 5:1-5).

1 Corinthians Chapter 4

1 Corinthians 4:1-5   Paul And Apollos Are Servants Of Christ

¹ So then, think of us as Christ's servants and stewards of God's mysteries. ² Here, moreover, it is required of stewards that they be found faithful. ³ But with me it is a very small thing that I should be judged by you, or by a human court. Yes, I do not even judge myself. 4 For I know nothing against myself. Yet I am not justified by this, but he who judges me is the Lord. ⁵ Therefore, judge nothing before the time, until the Lord comes, who will both bring to light the hidden things of darkness and reveal the counsels of the hearts. Then each man will get his praise from God.

4:1-2. The people in Corinth tended to elevate their favorite leader. "I follow Paul, I follow Apollos, I follow Cephas." Paul speaks the truth when he says that all ministers of Christ, including apostles, are mere servants and stewards.

Let's look at these terms:

Servant: one who serves another person. The servant works for the benefit of the person being served. The servant receives no glory for their work.

Steward: one who is entrusted to take care of another person's wealth or resources. The steward follows the owner's direction and preserves or distributes resources according to the instructions given. See the Parable of the Talents; Matt. 25:14-30.

The mysteries of God: Salvation is the chief mystery of God. Paul, Apollos, and Cephas preached the gospel because they were servants of Christ, and they were stewards of the mystery of the gospel. "Assuming that you have heard of the stewardship of God's grace that was given to me for you" (Eph 3:2).

16

Think about it!

What is grace, and how can one be a steward of God's grace? When God uses you to speak peace and love into someone's life, you are being an instrument to deliver grace. (1 Peter 4:10

4:3-5. There were some people in Corinth who disputed Paul's apostleship (2 Cor. 11:5). Paul asserts that no one has the right to judge him, and in fact, he does not sit in judgment on himself. His conscience is clear before God. Because he is a servant and a steward, only his master has the right to judge him. When the Lord returns, he himself will judge his servants, and each person will receive his reward from God.

Questions:

The factious leaders in Corinth judged Paul's ministry by saying that he was inferior to them. Supposedly, he was not an eloquent speaker. He did not use Greek rhetoric or words of human wisdom. On what basis will Paul be judged when he stands before God as a servant? See 1 Cor. 3:10-15.

1 Corinthians 4:8-13   True Apostles Are Willing To Suffer

[8] You are already filled. You have already become rich. You have come to reign without us. Yes, and I wish that you did reign, that we also might reign with you! [9] For I think that God has put us apostles on display last of all, like men sentenced to death. For we are made a spectacle to the world, both to angels and men. [10] We are fools for Christ's sake, but you are wise in Christ. We are weak, but you are strong. You have honor, but we have dishonor. [11] Even to this present hour, we hunger, thirst, are naked, are beaten, and have no certain dwelling place. [12] We toil, working with our own hands. When people curse us, we bless. Being persecuted, we endure. [13] Being defamed, we entreat. We are made as the filth of the world, useless scum, even until now.

4:8. Corinth was a complex church. Although many of the people were middle or working class, the church still had a fair amount of pride as each person claimed a certain level of status. Some of this pride may have come from their association with spiritual gifts. Spiritual gifts belong to those who are servants of Christ and stewards of the divine mysteries; gifts should not lead to spiritual pride.

4:9-13. True apostles are servants and willing to suffer for Christ. Rather than being prideful, they are willing to be treated like useless scum.

Questions:

What would you think of someone who claimed to have great spiritual gifts, but used them for their own personal gain?

In what ways was Paul Christ-like?

1 Corinthians 4:14-21   Paul as a Spiritual Father

[14] I do not write these things to shame you, but to admonish you as my beloved children. [15] For though you have ten thousand teachers in Christ, you do not have many fathers. For in Christ Jesus, I became your father through the gospel. [16] I beg you, therefore, be imitators of me. [17] Because of this, I have sent Timothy to you, who is my beloved and faithful son in the Lord, who will remind you of my ways which are in Christ, even as I teach everywhere in every assembly. [18] Now some are puffed up, as though I were not coming to you. [19] But I will come to you shortly, if the Lord is willing. And I will know, not the word of those who are puffed up, but the power. [20] For God's Kingdom is not in word, but in power. [21] What do you want? Shall I come to you with a rod, or in love and a spirit of gentleness?

4:14-17. Paul again is forced to defend his role as an apostle. He is not only a teacher, but a spiritual father.

4:18-21. Paul is planning another visit to Corinth, and when he comes, he will not be impressed with those who are puffed up with pride, but he wants to know what power they have; "for God's Kingdom is not in word, but in power."

Paul's power is in his message. "For the message of the cross is foolishness to those who are perishing, but to us who are being saved it is the power of God." (1 Cor 1:18 NIV).

Reflection:

Paul performed miracles, and sometimes those miracles led people to Christ. (See Acts 24:1-6). However, to the Church at Corinth, where the people boasted in spiritual gifts, Paul did not boast in his own gifts; he relied upon the power of the message of the cross.

1 Corinthians Chapter 5

1 Corinthians 5:1-5   Sin and Church Discipline

[1] It is actually reported that there is sexual immorality among you, and such sexual immorality as is not even named among the Gentiles, that one is sleeping with his father's wife. [2] You are arrogant, and did not mourn instead, that he who had done this deed might be removed from among you. [3] Although I am not present in body, I am certainly present in spirit, and I have already judged him who has done this thing. [4] In the name of our Lord Jesus Christ, when you are gathered together, and my spirit is present with the power of our Lord Jesus Christ, [5] you are to deliver such a one to Satan for the destruction of his flesh, that the spirit may be saved in the day of the Lord Jesus.

5:1-3. Paul began this letter by addressing the people as the "saints of God." Then, in chapter 3, he said that they are spiritually immature. Now he goes into more detail; there is sexual immorality in the church. Remember that the people of Corinth had a mixed background. Some were Jews and had been under the Law of Moses, but many of the others came from pagan backgrounds. Paul had heard reports (see 1 Cor. 1:11) that they were tolerating immorality so bad that it would violate even pagan standards, and it certainly violated the Law of Moses (Lev. 18:8, 20:11).

Reason why the church must deal with sin among its members

1) To tolerate sin sends the wrong message about the gospel, and other members will think that it is acceptable.
2) Dealing with sin is necessary to protect the congregation. Sin often spreads to others.
3) Dealing with the sin may bring the guilty person to repentance.
4) Dealing with sin may be necessary to protect the victims.

5:4-5. Turn the person over to Satan! Paul is advocating that the church allow Satan to bring harm to the person's body to bring them to repentance. People in the church have some measure of protection from Satan. The church has the authority to remove that protection, which opens the person to spiritual attacks from the enemy.

Note: some commentators think that "destruction of the flesh" (v. 5) refers to his fleshly spirit. Paul does use the term that way in some cases, but it is hard to see how Satan could (or would) destroy a person's worldly spirit.

Reflection!

This is a very unusual verse of Scripture. What are your thoughts? See Titus 3:10.

1 Corinthians 5:9-13   Sin and Church Discipline – Part 2

[9] I wrote to you in my letter to have no company with sexual sinners; [10] yet not at all meaning with the sexual sinners of this world, or with the covetous and extortionists, or with idolaters, for then you would have to leave the world. [11] But as it is, I wrote to you not to associate with anyone who is called a brother who is a sexual sinner, or covetous, or an idolater, or a slanderer, or a drunkard, or an extortionist. Do not even eat with such a person. [12] For what do I have to do with also judging those who are outside? Do you not judge those who are within? [13] But those who are outside, God judges. "Put away the wicked man from among yourselves."

5:9-11. We only have two of Paul's letters to Corinth in our Bibles, but he makes reference to a previous letter. Unfortunately, that letter has not been preserved. There was also a letter from the church to Paul, and it also no longer exists (1 Cor. 7:1).

5:9-13. We now receive some additional teachings about church discipline.

Church discipline is for those in the church! We are not called to judge those outside of the church.

Questions:

If my neighbor sins and I know about it, should I confront him?

When do we confront people in the church? What level of sin requires action? What about gluttony? What about immodest dress attire? What about a person who drinks to excess? (See the reasons why the church must deal with sin on the previous page.)

How do you respond to people who say, "We are all sinners, do not judge people, leave them to God"?

When do we "put away the wicked man…" (v. 13)

1 Corinthians Chapter 6

1 Corinthians 6:1-8   Lawsuits Among Believers

¹ Dare any of you, having a matter against his neighbor, go to law before the unrighteous, and not before the saints? ² Do you not know that the saints will judge the world? And if the world is judged by you, are you unworthy to judge the smallest matters? ³ Do you not know that we will judge angels? How much more, things that pertain to this life? ⁴ If then you have to judge things pertaining to this life, do you set them to judge who are of no account in the assembly? ⁵ I say this to move you to shame. Is there not even one wise man among you who would be able to decide between his brothers? ⁶ But brother goes to law with brother, and that before unbelievers! ⁷ Therefore, you are already defeated in that you have lawsuits one with another. Why not rather be wronged? Why not rather be defrauded? ⁸ No, but you yourselves do wrong and defraud, and that against your brothers.

6:1-6. Paul is still talking about divisions in the church. Here, he lays out a key principle for resolving conflict. Whenever possible, conflicts between members of the church should be handled by members of the church; we should not take fellow believers to court. This assumes that all parties to the conflict are believers.

"If your brother sins against you, go, show him his fault between you and him alone. If he listens to you, you have gained back your brother. But if he does not listen, take one or two more with you, so that at the mouth of two or three witnesses every word may be established. If he refuses to listen to them, tell it to the church. If he refuses to hear the church, let him be to you as a Gentile or a tax collector." **Matt. 18:15-17**

6:2-3. We will the world… and we will judge angels. Probably means that we will judge them during the millennial reign, and we will judge the fallen angels (2 Peter 2:4). There are no other references to this in Scripture.

6:7-8. Paul is always concerned about unity in the church and preserving the witness of the church in the world.

Questions:

If Christians take each other to court, how does that dispute tarnish the reputation of the church?

On what basis would the civil courts decide the case before them? On what basis would the Christian leaders decide the merits of the case?

1 Corinthians 6:9-11   The Unrighteous will not Inherit the Kingdom of God

[9] Or do you not know that the unrighteous will not inherit God's Kingdom? Do not be deceived. Neither the sexually immoral, nor idolaters, nor adulterers, nor male prostitutes, nor homosexuals, [10] nor thieves, nor covetous, nor drunkards, nor slanderers, nor extortionists, will inherit God's Kingdom. [11] Some of you were such, but you were washed. You were sanctified. You were justified in the name of the Lord Jesus, and in the Spirit of our God.

6:9-11. The protestant church is built on the foundation of salvation by grace through faith, not by works (Eph. 2:8). Sometimes that is taken to mean that a Christian can sin without limit and still enter heaven. Paul defeats that argument by listing several examples of people who will not be admitted into God's kingdom.

Paul told us in the previous chapter (5:9-13) that we are not to judge those outside of the church, but our concern is with those who profess to be believers. Since some of the people in Corinth came from pagan backgrounds with very little understanding of Christian standards, he gives examples of unacceptable behavior. Notice that he includes covetousness and drunkards in the same list as homosexuality and prostitutes.

Reflection!

Are all of the sins that Paul listed equal in the eyes of God?

How do you define sin?

1 Corinthians 6:12-20   Flee Sexual Immorality!

[12] All things are lawful for me, but not all things are beneficial. All things are lawful for me, but I will not be brought under the power of anything. [13] Foods for the belly, and the belly for foods, but God will bring to nothing both it and them. But the body is not for sexual immorality, but for the Lord, and the Lord for the body. [14] Now God raised up the Lord, and will also raise us up by his power. [15] Do you not know that your bodies are members of Christ? Shall I then take the members of Christ and make them members of a prostitute? May it never be! [16] Or do you not know that he who is joined to a prostitute is one body? For, "The two", he says, "will become one flesh." [17] But he who is joined to the Lord is one spirit. [18] Flee sexual immorality! "Every sin that a man does is outside the body," but he who commits sexual immorality sins against his own body. [19] Or do you not know that your body is a temple of the Holy Spirit who is in you, whom you have from God? You are not your own, [20] for you were bought with a price. Therefore glorify God in your body and in your spirit, which are God's.

6:12-14. The translation of verse 12 is complicated. Older translations assume that Paul is saying, "all things are lawful for me, but not all things are beneficial." Newer translations assume that Paul is quoting the Corinthians, and then he refutes their sayings.

"I have the right to do anything," you say—but not everything is beneficial. "I have the right to do anything"—but I will not be mastered by anything. (NIV).

Paul's point is this: Even if there is no specific biblical command, if something is spiritually harmful for you, you must avoid it.

John Wesley's mother defined sin in these terms:

> "Whatever weakens your reasoning, impairs the tenderness of your conscience, obscures your sense of God, or takes away your relish for spiritual things, in short, if anything increases the authority of the flesh over the spirit, that to you becomes sin, however good it is in itself." – Susanna Wesley –

6:15-20. Paul previously told us that our bodies (plural) are the temple of God (singular) (1 Cor. 3:16), and now he uses the same metaphor to describe the individual Christian. When a man and woman get married, they become one flesh (Matt, 19:5). So it is, a person who sleeps with a prostitute becomes one with the prostitute (v. 15-16). Your body has been pledged to God in marriage; he has purchased you (redeemed you from sin). You become a temple (dwelling place) of God. You sin against that dwelling place of God when you commit sexual immorality.

Question:

6:20-21. What does the Scripture mean when it says, "You are not your own, you were bought with a price?

1 Corinthians Chapter 7

1 Corinthians 7:1-9   Marriage Relationships

¹ Now concerning the things about which you wrote to me: it is good for a man not to touch a woman. ² But, because of sexual immorality, let each man have his own wife, and let each woman have her own husband. ³ Let the husband give his wife the affection owed to her, and likewise also the wife her husband. ⁴ The wife does not have authority over her own body, but the husband does. Likewise, the husband does not have authority over his own body, but the wife does. ⁵ Do not deprive one another, unless it is by consent for a season, that you may give yourselves to fasting and prayer, and then come together again, that Satan does not tempt you because of your lack of self-control.

⁶ But this I say by way of concession, not of commandment. ⁷ Yet I wish that all men were like me. However, each man has his own gift from God, one of this kind, and another of that kind. ⁸ But I say to the unmarried and to widows, it is good for them if they remain even as I am. ⁹ But if they do not have self-control, let them marry, for it's better to marry than to burn with passion.

The church at Corinth had written to Paul concerning marriage relationships, and he addresses those questions in this chapter.

7:1-5. Husbands and wives should not withhold sexual relationships from each other. "Let the husband give his wife the affection owed her, and likewise also the wife her husband" (v. 3). Withholding this affection may give way for Satan to tempt one or both of the marriage partners.

7:6-9. Some people have the spiritual gift of celibacy. That is, they do not have the same sexual passions and needs as most other people. Paul places himself in that category, but he realizes that not everyone has the gift of celibacy.

Question:

It is better to marry than to burn [with passion]. The words "with passion" have been added by most translations to add clarity. A few commentators take the verse to mean it is better to marry than to burn in hell, but that does not fit Paul's theology. What do you think it means?

1 Corinthians 7:10-16   Marriage and Unbelieving Spouses

[10] But to the married I command—not I, but the Lord—that the wife should not leave her husband, [11] but if she departs, let her remain unmarried, or else be reconciled to her husband; similarly, I also command that the husband not leave his wife.

[12] But to the rest I—not the Lord—say, if any brother has an unbelieving wife, and she is content to live with him, let him not leave her. [13] The woman who has an unbelieving husband, and he is content to live with her, let her not leave her husband. [14] For the unbelieving husband is sanctified in the wife, and the unbelieving wife is sanctified in the husband. Otherwise, your children would be unclean, but now they are holy. [15] Yet if the unbeliever departs, let there be separation. The brother or the sister is not under bondage in such cases, but God has called us in peace. [16] For how do you know, wife, whether you will save your husband? Or how do you know, husband, whether you will save your wife?

7:11. A believer who is married to an unbeliever should not divorce the unbeliever just because the spouse is a non-believer. If the unbeliever is willing to live in peace with the believer, they should remain married.

7:14. The believing spouse brings a measure of God's grace and protection in the home. The unbeliever is sanctified (set apart) and covered by that protection, as are the children. "Your children are holy" (v. 14). This does not mean that the unbeliever and the children are saved based on their relationship to the believer, but they are covered by a covenant. "Paul teaches that the sanctification of the believing partner extends to the unbeliever."[1] As an additional benefit, the believer's influence may lead to the unbeliever's salvation.

7:15 God has called us to live in peace. Living together in peace is the key to a successful marriage relationship. If the unbeliever causes extreme tension or harm, the believer is not required to stay in the relationship.

If the unbeliever departs, "The brother or the sister is not under bondage in such cases." There are different opinions on what this means, but the apparent meaning is that the innocent party is free from the marriage contract and may remarry.[2] Paul uses the same "bound" versus "not bound" later in the chapter. "A wife is bound by law for as long as her husband lives; but if the husband is dead, she is free to be married to whomever she desires, only in the Lord" (7:39). In verse 15, Paul says that a believer is not bound if their unbelieving spouse leaves the marriage.

1 Corinthians 7:17-24   Your Current Condition

[17] Only, as the Lord has distributed to each man, as God has called each, so let him walk. So I command in all the churches. [18] Was anyone called having been circumcised? Let him not become uncircumcised. Has anyone been called while uncircumcised? Let him not be circumcised. [19] Circumcision is nothing, and uncircumcision is nothing, but what matters is keeping God's commandments. [20] Let each man stay in that calling in which he was called. [21] Were you called while a slave? Do not let that bother you, but if you get an opportunity to become free, use it. [22] For the one who was called in the Lord while being a slave is the Lord's

---

[1] Leon Morris, *1 Corinthians* (Grand Rapids, Inter-Varsity Press, 1983), 110.

[2] Keener holds that the innocent party may remarry. Craig Keener, *1-2 Corinthians* (Cambridge: Cambridge Univ. Press, 2005), 65. Fee holds that the innocent party is not free to remarry but is not bound to maintain the marriage relationship. Gordon Fee, *The First Epistle to the Corinthians*, The New International Commentary on the New Testament (Grand Rapids: Eerdmans, 1987), 302-303.

free man. Likewise, he who was called being free is Christ's slave. [23] You were bought with a price. Do not become slaves of men. [24] Brothers, let each man, in whatever condition he was called, stay in that condition with God.

7:17-24. The church at Corinth was very diverse and included Jews (circumcised men), Greeks (uncircumcised), and slaves. Paul wants to assure them that these differences do not affect their relationship with Christ. "There is neither Jew nor Greek, there is neither slave nor free man, there is neither male nor female; for you are all one in Christ Jesus" (Gal. 3:28).

Throughout his letters, Paul works towards unity in the church. Women and slaves were in subservient positions in Paul's time. It is Paul's position that it is better to remain in such positions if that is what is required to maintain unity in the church. If a slave can gain their freedom, they should do so, but if they cannot, their position as a slave does not affect their position with God. This is all about maintaining unity and peace in the church.

Question: Our culture has changed, and women and slaves are no longer required to be subservient in order to maintain peace. Would Paul give the same advice today?

1 Corinthians 7:25-35   Should Ministers Get Married?

²⁵ Now concerning virgins, I have no commandment from the Lord, but I give my judgment as one who has obtained mercy from the Lord to be trustworthy. ²⁶ Therefore, I think that because of the distress that is on us, it's good for a man to remain as he is. ²⁷ Are you bound to a wife? Do not seek to be freed. Are you free from a wife? Do not seek a wife. ²⁸ But if you marry, you have not sinned. If a virgin marries, she has not sinned. Yet such will have distress in the flesh, and I want to spare you. ²⁹ But I say this, brothers: the time is short. From now on, both those who have wives may be as though they had none; ³⁰ and those who weep, as though they did not weep; and those who rejoice, as though they did not rejoice; and those who buy, as though they did not possess; ³¹ and those who use the world, as not using it to the fullest, because the present form of this world is passing away.

³² But I desire to have you to be free from care. He who is unmarried is concerned for the things of the Lord, how he may please the Lord; ³³ but he who is married is concerned about the things of the world, how he may please his wife. ³⁴ There is also a difference between a wife and a virgin. The unmarried woman cares about the things of the Lord, that she may be holy both in body and in spirit. But she who is married cares about the things of the world—how she may please her husband. ³⁵ This I say for your own benefit, not that I may ensnare you, but for that which is appropriate, and that you may attend to the Lord without distraction.

7:25-35. Paul repeats what he said previously in verses 6-9. He urges people not to get married, but he recognizes that not everyone has the gift of celibacy.

In verse 29, Paul seems to indicate that he expected Christ to return very soon (in his lifetime), and he urges Christian ministers to remain unmarried if they can. Speaking of the return of Christ, Paul included himself in those who will still be alive (1 Thess. 4:17). Thessalonians and 1 Corinthians were among Paul's earliest writings. However, in 2

Timothy, written about 13 years later while in prison, Paul is told that he will soon die (2 Tim. 4:6-8).

Question:

Is Paul saying that ministers should not get married? If so, was this based on a situation peculiar to his day and time?

1 Corinthians Chapter 8

1 Corinthians 8:1-6   Eating Meat Offered to Idols

¹ Now concerning things sacrificed to idols: We know that we all have knowledge. Knowledge puffs up, but love builds up. ² But if anyone thinks that he knows anything, he does not yet know as he ought to know. ³ But anyone who loves God is known by him.

⁴ Therefore concerning the eating of things sacrificed to idols, we know that no idol is anything in the world, and that there is no other God but one. ⁵ For though there are things that are called "gods", whether in the heavens or on earth—as there are many "gods" and many "lords"— ⁶ yet to us there is one God, the Father, of whom are all things, and we for him; and one Lord, Jesus Christ, through whom are all things, and we live through him.

8:1-6. The pagan religions offered sacrifices to their idol gods. Meat that was left over after the sacrifice was sold in the public meat markets. This was evidently a big concern in Corinth because Paul covered it twice in this letter. It is covered here in chapter 8, and again in chapter 10 (vs. 19-33).

The subject of meat offered to idols is covered in more detail in chapter 10, and so we will provide comments there.

1 Corinthians Chapter 9

1 Corinthians 9:1-12 A Defense of Paul's Apostleship

¹ Am I not free? Am I not an apostle? Have I not seen Jesus Christ, our Lord? Are you not my work in the Lord? ² If to others I am not an apostle, yet at least I am to you; for you are the seal of my apostleship in the Lord.

³ My defense to those who examine me is this: ⁴ Have we no right to eat and to drink? ⁵ Have we no right to take along a wife who is a believer, even as the rest of the apostles, and the brothers of the Lord, and Cephas? ⁶ Or have only Barnabas and I no right to not work? ⁷ What soldier ever serves at his own expense? Who plants a vineyard, and does not eat of its fruit? Or who feeds a flock, and does not drink from the flock's milk?

⁸ Do I speak these things according to the ways of men? Or does the law not also say the same thing? ⁹ For it is written in the law of Moses, "You shall not muzzle an ox while it treads out the grain." Is it for the oxen that God cares, ¹⁰ or does he say it assuredly for our sake? Yes, it was written for our sake, because he who plows ought to plow in hope, and he who threshes in hope should partake of his hope. ¹¹ If we sowed to you spiritual things, is it a great thing if we reap your fleshly things? ¹² If others partake of this right over you, do not we yet more? Nevertheless, we did not use this right, but we bear all things, that we may cause no hindrance to the gospel of Christ.

Paul has had a long-running dispute with certain men in Corinth who considered themselves apostles, and they argued that Paul was not a true apostle. See 2 Cor. 11-12.

9:1-2. The true test of an apostle is how the Holy Spirit works through them. Paul argues that he is a true apostle because of how the Spirit worked through him to bring people to Christ in Corinth.

The Corinthian converts are "the seal of his apostleship" (v. 2).

9:3. It may seem strange that Paul should have to defend himself for not accepting a salary, but these false apostles were saying that Paul was simply a layman or a traveling bum because he did not accept a salary, had no wife, and did not demand support from the churches.[3]

9:4-11. Paul first argues that ministers have the right to get paid. He bases the argument on logic as well as Scripture.

Logically, soldiers are not required to work for free. Farmers are allowed to eat from their own vineyards and drink the milk from their flock. Paul's arguments rest on the fact that he founded the church at Corinth—he is their spiritual father.

From Scripture (v. 8-10), the OT says that "You shall not muzzle an ox while it treads out the grain." The ox is permitted to eat the grain while it is doing its work.

9:12. Although Paul had this right, "Nevertheless, we did not use this right, but we bear all things, that we may cause no hindrance to the gospel of Christ."

To us today, this whole argument may seem unnecessary. If Paul did not take advantage of his rights to be paid and have a wife, why does he have to start with a defense of why others deserve these rights? The answer lies in verse 3: "My defense to those who examine me is this." Paul's adversaries argued that he did not fit the general mold of an apostle, and yet, Paul did not want to disparage the other apostles, including Barnabas and Cephas.

---

[3] "It was accepted that an apostle ought to be maintained by those to whom he ministered." Leon Morris, *1 Corinthians*, 133.

1 Corinthians 9:19-23   I have become all things to all men

¹⁹ For though I was free from all, I brought myself under bondage
to all, that I might gain the more. ²⁰ To the Jews I became as a Jew,
that I might gain Jews; to those who are under the law, as under
the law, that I might gain those who are under the law; ²¹ to those
who are without law, as without law (not being without law toward
God, but under law toward Christ), that I might win those who are
without law. ²² To the weak I became as weak, that I might gain the
weak. I have become all things to all men, that I may by all means
save some. ²³ Now I do this for the sake of the gospel, that I may
be a joint partaker of it.

9:19-23. Paul is willing to sacrifice his personal rights and
preferences in order to win others to Christ. He does not
compromise his message, because the message of the cross is the
power of God unto salvation (1 Cor. 1:18).

"It is good to not eat meat, drink wine, nor do anything that makes
your brother stumble" (Rom. 14:21).

Paul taught the Gentiles that they did not need to be circumcised
(Gal 6), but when he was in Jerusalem (the church was primarily
Jewish Christians), he respected their custom to continue
circumcision (Acts 21).

9:22-23 I have become all things to all men, that I may by all means
save some. Now I do this for the sake of the gospel, that I may be a
joint partaker of it.

Question:

What are some of the things you do in your church or denomination
that are established customs, but are not required by the gospel?

Would you be willing to change if it would help more people come to
Christ?

What are some of the things that divide us? Race, culture, politics,
music?

1 Corinthians Chapter 10

1 Corinthians 10:1-11   Lessons from Israel's Journey

^{1} Now I would not have you ignorant, brothers, that our fathers were all under the cloud, and all passed through the sea; ^{2} and were all baptized into Moses in the cloud and in the sea; ^{3} and all ate the same spiritual food; ^{4} and all drank the same spiritual drink. For they drank of a spiritual rock that followed them, and the rock was Christ. ^{5} However, with most of them, God was not well pleased, for they were overthrown in the wilderness.

^{6} Now these things are useful examples for us, to the intent we should not lust after evil things as they also lusted. ^{7} Do not be idolaters, as some of them were. As it is written, "The people sat down to eat and drink, and rose up to play." ^{8} Let's not commit sexual immorality, as some of them committed, and in one day, twenty-three thousand fell. ^{9} Let's not test Christ, as some of them did and perished by the serpents. ^{10} Do not grumble, as some of them also grumbled, and perished by the destroyer. ^{11} Now all these things happened to them by way of example, and they were written for our admonition, on whom the ends of the ages have come.

10:1-11. Israel's journey from Egypt into Canaan is like the gospel in allegory. They were delivered from bondage (although they were reluctant to leave), they rebelled and complained about the journey, and they were reluctant to enter the promised land because they were afraid of the giants. Paul tells us that these things happened, not just for the benefit of the Israelites, but also as lessons for all people of all ages (vs. 6 & 11).

Questions:

Discuss your own Christian journey. What challenges have you faced? Can you describe a time when things did not go as you thought they would?

1 Corinthians 10:13-22   Temptations toward Idols

¹³ No temptation has taken you except what is common to man. God is faithful, who will not allow you to be tempted above what you are able, but will with the temptation also make a way of escape, that you may be able to endure it.

¹⁴ Therefore, my beloved, flee from idolatry. ¹⁵ I speak as to wise men. Judge what I say. ¹⁶ The cup of blessing which we bless, is it not a sharing of the blood of Christ? The bread which we break, is it not a sharing of the body of Christ? ¹⁷ Because there is one loaf of bread, we, who are many, are one body; for we all partake of the one loaf of bread. ¹⁸ Consider Israel according to the flesh. Do those who eat sacrifices not participate in the altar?

¹⁹ What am I saying then? That a thing sacrificed to idols is anything, or that an idol is anything? ²⁰ But I say that the things which the Gentiles sacrifice, they sacrifice to demons and not to God, and I do not desire that you would have fellowship with demons. ²¹ You cannot both drink the cup of the Lord and the cup of demons. You cannot both partake of the table of the Lord and of the table of demons. ²² Or do we provoke the Lord to jealousy? Are we stronger than he?

10:1-4. Corinth was a pagan city, and most of the Greeks worshiped idols. Those who came into the church had questions about how to live within their culture. Paul had just told them (chapter 9) to become all things to all people in order to win them to Christ.

10:19-22. Those who sacrifice to idols are actually sacrificing to demons, and they are participating in demon worship. This is a different situation than what Paul considers in 8:4-6.

Question:

Some were tempted to worship idols, perhaps because that was the way of their culture. Many of them had family members who still worshipped in the idol temples. Should they go to temple worship with their family members?

To understand and apply the gospel, we need to extract the principle truths from their original context and reapply them to our own. Would you go to a Hindu Temple for a celebration because a friend or family member asked you to attend with them?

1 Corinthians 10:23-33   Food Offered to Idols

[23] "All things are lawful for me," but not all things are profitable. "All things are lawful for me," but not all things build up. [24] Let no one seek his own, but each one his neighbor's good. [25] Whatever is sold in the butcher shop, eat, asking no question for the sake of conscience, [26] for "the earth is the Lord's, and its fullness." [27] But if one of those who do not believe invites you to a meal, and you are inclined to go, eat whatever is set before you, asking no questions for the sake of conscience. [28] But if anyone says to you, "This was offered to idols," do not eat it for the sake of the one who told you, and for the sake of conscience. For "the earth is the Lord's, with all its fullness." [29] Conscience, I say, not your own, but the other's conscience. For why is my liberty judged by another conscience? [30] If I partake with thankfulness, why am I denounced for something I give thanks for?

[31] Whether therefore you eat or drink, or whatever you do, do all to the glory of God. [32] Give no occasion for stumbling, whether to Jews, to Greeks, or to the assembly of God; [33] even as I also please all men in all things, not seeking my own profit, but the profit of the many, that they may be saved.

10:23. This section parallels chapter 8. You may want to review that section.

10:25-30. The pagan religions offered sacrifices to their idol gods. Meat that was left over after the sacrifice was sold in the public meat markets. (See also 1 Cor. 8:4-6).

Earlier in this chapter (vs. 14-22), Paul explicitly told the people not to participate in sacrificing to idols. But now he confronts a different problem. What about the meat that is left over after the sacrifices? Is the meat contaminated?

10:25. Paul says that idols are nothing at all. They are just pieces of wood and metal. The meat has not been contaminated. However, if someone who is eating the meat thinks of it as part of the idol sacrifice, then for that person, eating the meat would be sinful because they are identifying it with idols.

So, what are we to do? In chapter 9, Paul says that we are to become all things to all people. It's okay to eat meat purchased in the public market, and you do not need to ask where it came from. **(v. 28)** But if someone invites you to dinner, and they tell you that the meat came from the temple, you should not eat the meat. Not because it's contaminated, but to clear the conscience of the other person.

10:31-33. Whether therefore you eat or drink, or whatever you do, do all to the glory of God. Give no occasion for stumbling, whether to Jews, to Greeks, or to the church of God; even as I also please all men in all things, not seeking my own profit, but the profit of the many, that they may be saved.

Paul has said repeatedly that he is willing to sacrifice his own rights in order to win others to Christ.

Questions:

If I know that the meat is not contaminated, why not eat it? Maybe I should just educate the uninformed friends and go ahead and eat. How would Paul respond to that?

1 Corinthians Chapter 11

1 Corinthians 11:1-10   Hair and Head Coverings

[1] Be imitators of me, even as I also am of Christ.

[2] Now I praise you, brothers, that you remember me in all things, and hold firm the traditions, even as I delivered them to you. [3] But I would have you know that the head of every man is Christ, and the head of the woman is man, and the head of Christ is God. [4] Every man praying or prophesying, having his head covered, dishonors his head. [5] But every woman praying or prophesying with her head uncovered dishonors her head. For it is one and the same thing as if she were shaved. [6] For if a woman is not covered, let her hair also be cut off. But if it is shameful for a woman to have her hair cut off or be shaved, let her be covered. [7] For a man indeed ought not to have his head covered, because he is the image and glory of God, but the woman is the glory of the man. [8] For man is not from woman, but woman from man; [9] for man was not created for the woman, but woman for the man. [10] For this cause the woman ought to have a symbol of authority on her head, because of the angels.

11:2-3. One of the hardest things about Biblical interpretation is knowing what is based on the cultural conditions of the time, and what is eternal principles. Or, said another way, what eternal principles can we draw from each section of the text, regardless of the original context?

The Greek word for head is <u>kephale,</u> and it can mean the literal head, authority, or source. In the hierarchy, God is the head of Christ, Christ is the head of every man, and a husband is the head of his wife. The traditional interpretation is that the husband is the authority over his wife, just as Christ is the authority over every person. Other commentaries take the meaning of head to be the source: Christ is the source of life for mankind, and man is the source of woman (Adam was the source of Eve).

Two terms are important to understand:

Complementarian means that men and women are equal, but they have different but complementary roles in the home and church.

Egalitarian means that men and women are equal and each can take on any role in the church or home without distinction

Issue #1.

In what way is the husband the head of his wife?

In the complementarian view, the man (or husband) is assigned a role of leadership and is to exercise authority over his wife. Of course, following biblical principles, the husband must love his wife as Christ loved the church (Eph. 5:25).

In the egalitarian view, "head" means source, not authority.

Issue #2.

What does it mean for the woman to have her head covered, and why?

The literal interpretation is that women should wear a headcover of some sort—a hat or scarf. In Paul's day, if a woman went outside of her home without a head covering, she would be considered a prostitute.

Symbolically, some take "head covering" to mean authority—but not in a literal way. Head covering could also be a reference to her hair (v 6). For a woman to have short hair was also a sign of being a prostitute in Paul's time.

NIV… have authority over her own head.

ESV, NASB … have a symbol of authority over her head.

Culturally, women should not appear to be prostitutes when they are in church or out in public.

11:6. But if it is shameful for a woman to have her hair cut off or be shaved, let her be covered. There is a strong sense in which this is primarily a cultural argument. "If it is shameful..." In today's culture, it is not shameful for a woman to have short hair. So, are Paul's admonitions about hair and the sign of authority limited to his own day and time? It would seem that Paul's concern is that both men and women behave in a way that honors Christ; they should not send the wrong message to the people around them. Back to Paul's message, do not do anything that would cause someone else to stumble (9:22; Rom. 14:21).

11:10. Because of the angels. Paul implies that the angels are observing our behavior to learn about life under grace.

1 Corinthians 11:11-16   Hair – Part 2

[11] Nevertheless, neither is the woman independent of the man, nor the man independent of the woman, in the Lord. [12] For as woman came from man, so a man also comes through a woman; but all things are from God. [13] Judge for yourselves. Is it appropriate that a woman pray to God uncovered? [14] Does not even nature itself teach you that if a man has long hair, it is a dishonor to him? [15] But if a woman has long hair, it is a glory to her, for her hair is given to her for a covering. [16] But if any man seems to be contentious, we have no such custom, neither do the churches of God.

11:11. Now Paul exhibits a more conciliatory tone. For those who want to argue about the length of hair and who has authority over who, remember that men and women are both dependent upon each other.

11:13-14. Again, Paul bases his argument on what is appropriate. But appropriate based on what standard? It seems that Paul's biggest concern is that the church should send a clear message to the world about morality. Do not dress like a prostitute (male or female), and be willing to sacrifice your own rights for the good of others.

11:14. Long hair on a man. This is puzzling because there are no known teachings in Judaism or early Christianity against men having long hair. This is another indicator that some of Paul's teaching was based on local and cultural conditions. See verse 16.

11:16. "But if any man seems to be contentious, we have no such custom, neither do the churches of God." This verse is hard to translate. Did Paul really say, "we have no such custom," or did he say, "we have no other custom"?

NIV: We have no other practice

NASB2020: We have no such practice

NASB1995: We have no other practice

ESV: We have no such practice

Did Paul just negate his whole argument, or make it based on cultural circumstances?

1 Corinthians 11:20-34   Lord's Supper

[20] When, therefore, you assemble yourselves together, it is not the Lord's supper that you eat. [21] For in your eating, each one takes his own supper first. One is hungry, and another is drunk. [22] What, do you not have houses to eat and drink in? Or do you despise God's assembly and put them to shame who do not have enough? What shall I tell you? Shall I praise you? In this, I do not praise you.

[23] For I received from the Lord that which also I delivered to you, that the Lord Jesus on the night in which he was betrayed took bread. [24] When he had given thanks, he broke it and said, "Take, eat. This is my body, which is broken for you. Do this in memory of me." [25] In the same way, he also took the cup after supper, saying, "This cup is the new covenant in my blood. Do this, as often as you drink, in memory of me." [26] For as often as you eat this bread and drink this cup, you proclaim the Lord's death until he comes.

[27] Therefore, whoever eats this bread or drinks the Lord's cup in a way unworthy of the Lord will be guilty of the body and the blood of the Lord. [28] But let a man examine himself, and so let him eat of the bread and drink of the cup. [29] For he who eats and drinks in an unworthy way eats and drinks judgment to himself if he does not discern the Lord's body. [30] For this cause many among you are weak and sickly, and not a few sleep. [31] For if we discerned ourselves, we would not be judged. [32] But when we are judged, we are disciplined by the Lord, that we may not be condemned with the world. [33] Therefore, my brothers, when you come together to eat, wait for one another. [34] But if anyone is hungry, let him eat at home, lest your coming together be for judgment. The rest I will set in order whenever I come.

11:20-22. The church of the first century held "love feasts" (agapa feasts), which were like church potlucks. The love feasts were also "commemoration meals" to celebrate the Lord's last supper with his disciples. At the love feasts, people often ate and drank to excess, and the poor did not receive their share. Paul chides them: "This is not the Lord's Supper!'"

11:23. Paul was not present for the original Lord's supper, but he says that what he knows about it came by way of revelation from the Lord.

The drink represents the shed blood of Christ. The broken bread represents the broken body of Christ as it hung on the cross.

There are two principal views of the meaning of the Lord's supper, which is also called Holy Communion or the Eucharist. The two elements represent the death of Christ, who paid the price for our sins. Jesus also said that the blood represents the new covenant in his blood.

The symbolic view is that it is a reminder for the believer of what Christ has done for us. It does not make any change in believers.

The means of grace view (Methodist, Lutheran, early Baptist) is that God uses the Lord's supper as an instrument to strengthen the life of the believer. It does not directly result in the forgiveness of sins.

The sacramental view (Catholic) is that God forgives sins as a result of the Eucharist. Taking the Eucharist is always effective and is not dependent on the individual's faith.

John Piper summarizes the means of grace position as it was confirmed by the Second London Baptist Confession of Faith (1677/1688).

"Christ instituted the Lord's Supper for five reasons… The Supper serves as a vivid reminder of and witness to the sacrificial death of Christ. Then, participation in the Lord's Supper enables believers to grasp more firmly all that Christ has done for them through his death on the cross. In this way, the Lord's Supper is a means of spiritual nourishment and growth. Fourth, the Lord's Supper serves as a time when believers recommit themselves to Christ. Finally, the Lord's Supper affirms the indissoluble union that exists, on the one hand, between Christ and believers, and, on the other, between individual believers."[4]

---

[4] John Piper, "A Meal for the Journey," https://www.desiringgod.org/articles/a-meal-for-the-journey

11:27-29. What does Paul mean by "in a way unworthy of the Lord" and "to discern the Lord's body"? Clearly, he has condemned their manner of eating and drinking to excess, while giving to the rich and neglecting the poor. Beyond that, he says that they have failed to discern the Lord's body. There are two possible meanings. One is that they fail to recognize that the food represents Christ's broken and crucified body on the cross. If this love feast is truly to commemorate Christ's death and the last supper, then the food is his body. The second possible meaning is that the church is the body of Christ, and by neglecting the poor, they are mistreating their fellow believers in the body of Christ.

11:30-32. Because of their sin, some of the people at Corinth suffered physical sickness and even death because of their offenses against the body of Christ.

Questions:

What is your understanding of the Lord's Supper?

What is the tradition of your church? How does your church prepare the people for the Lord's Supper?

1 Corinthians Chapter 12

1 Corinthians 12:1-9   About Spiritual Gifts

¹ Now concerning spiritual things, brothers, I do not want you to be uninformed. ² You know that when you were pagans, you were led away to those mute idols, however you might be led. ³ Therefore, I make known to you that no man speaking by God's Spirit says, "Jesus is accursed," and no one can say, "Jesus is Lord," except by the Holy Spirit.

⁴ Now there are various kinds of gifts, but the same Spirit. ⁵ There are various kinds of service, and the same Lord. ⁶ There are various kinds of workings, but the same God who works all things in all. ⁷ But to each one is given the manifestation of the Spirit for the profit of all. ⁸ For to one is given through the Spirit the word of wisdom, and to another the word of knowledge according to the same Spirit, ⁹ to another faith by the same Spirit, and to another gifts of healings by the same Spirit, ¹⁰ and to another workings of miracles, and to another prophecy, and to another discerning of spirits, to another different kinds of languages, and to another the interpretation of languages. ¹¹ But the one and the same Spirit produces all of these, giving to each one separately as he desires.

12:1-3. The Church at Corinth had a full range of spiritual gifts, but they lacked understanding of how to use the gifts for the good of the church. Paul asserts that you cannot separate God the Spirit from Jesus, the Son of God. If you do not recognize that Jesus is of God, you will not understand the things of the Spirit.

12:14-11. Gifts of the Spirit are the actions of the Spirit through a human individual. The gifts listed in 1 Corinthians Chapter 12 are examples of the gifts, but not an exhaustive list. Any supernatural work of the Spirit through an individual is a spiritual gift. Each gift is different, but it is the same Spirit that works the gift.

12:11. Distributing to each one as he [God] desires. God sovereignly gives spiritual gifts to people according to God's sovereign will. He provides the gifts according to the needs of his body, which is the church. We can desire and pray for certain gifts (1 Cor. 12:31; 14:1, 14:12-13), but God will make the final selection.

1 Corinthians 12:14-22 Gifts of the Spirit as Members of the Body

[14] For the body is not one member, but many. [15] If the foot says, "Because I'm not the hand, I'm not part of the body," it would not therefore cease being part of the body. [16] If the ear says, "Because I'm not the eye, I'm not part of the body," it would not therefore cease being of the body. [17] If the whole body were an eye, where would the hearing be? If the whole were hearing, where would the smelling be? [18] But now God has set the members, each one of them, in the body, just as he desired. [19] If they were all one member, where would the body be? [20] But now there are many members, but one body. [21] The eye cannot tell the hand, "I have no need for you," or again the head to the feet, "I have no need for you." [22] No, much rather, those members of the body which seem to be weaker are necessary.

12:14-18. God arranges people with spiritual gifts according to the needs of the body—the church.

12:19. The body must have diversity. A healthy body needs many different kinds of gifted people.

12:21-22. Your spiritual gift was not given to you for your own good, but for the good of others. Each member of the body of Christ must serve the other members; there is no room for pride or arrogance. We are all servants one to another.

Question:

In what ways is a church like a human body in terms of the diversity of its gifts, like the parts of the human body? Explain Paul's analogy.

1 Corinthians 12:23-31 Gifts of the Spirit as Members of the Body

²³ Those parts of the body which we think to be less honorable, on those we bestow more abundant honor; and our unpresentable parts have more abundant modesty, ²⁴ while our presentable parts have no such need. But God composed the body together, giving more abundant honor to the inferior part, ²⁵ that there should be no division in the body, but that the members should have the same care for one another. ²⁶ When one member suffers, all the members suffer with it. When one member is honored, all the members rejoice with it.

²⁷ Now you are the body of Christ, and members individually. ²⁸ God has placed some in the church: first apostles, second prophets, third teachers, then miracle workers, then gifts of healings, helps, governments, and various kinds of languages. ²⁹ Are all apostles? Are all prophets? Are all teachers? Are all miracle workers? ³⁰ Do all have gifts of healings? Do all speak in various languages? Do all interpret? ³¹ But earnestly desire the best gifts. Moreover, I show you a more excellent way.

12:23. We cannot all be eyes, or hands, or feet. Sometimes, a person with one gift may elevate that gift above others, as if their gift is the most important.

12:26. "When one member suffers, all the members suffer with it. When one member is honored, all the members rejoice with it." In the human body, if you have an earache, your whole body hurts. In the spiritual body, we all benefit from each other's gifts, and we are all worse off if a gifted person is missing from our fellowship.

12:28. Apostles, prophets, and other ministers. Sometimes Scripture may differentiate between a spiritual gift and the role of a minister. For example, an apostle probably has many gifts in order to fulfill their ministry.

There are several different lists of spiritual gifts.

Romans 12:6–8	1 Corinthians 12:8:10	Ephesians 4:11
Prophesying	Word of wisdom	Apostles
Serving	Word of knowledge	Prophets
Teaching	Faith	Evangelists
Encouraging	Gifts of healing	Pastors
Giving	Miracles	Teachers
Leading	Prophecy	
(Administration)	Discerning of spirits	
Showing mercy	Speaking in languages (tongues)	
	Interpretation of languages (tongues)	

The ministries listed in Ephesians are ministry callings and not singular gifts. For example, a pastor probably has the gifts of teaching and leadership, as well as the gift of compassion.

12:31. This chapter closes with Paul's admonition that we should "earnestly desire the best gifts." The "best gifts" are those that are most beneficial to the church. All spiritual gifts are from God, and all are good, but some are more beneficial to the church. "Since you are eager for gifts of the Spirit, try to excel in those that build up the church" (1 Cor. 14:12).

Questions:

What are your spiritual gifts?

What gifts would you like to have?

1 Corinthians Chapter 13

1 Corinthians 13:1-7   Love is the Most Important

[1] If I speak with the languages of men and of angels, but do not have love, I have become sounding brass or a clanging cymbal. [2] If I have the gift of prophecy, and know all mysteries and all knowledge, and if I have all faith, so as to remove mountains, but do not have love, I am nothing. [3] If I give away all my goods to feed the poor, and if I give my body to be burned, but do not have love, it profits me nothing.

[4] Love is patient and is kind. Love does not envy. Love does not brag, is not proud, [5] does not behave itself inappropriately, does not seek its own way, is not provoked, keeps no record of wrongs; [6] does not rejoice in unrighteousness, but rejoices with the truth; [7] bears all things, believes all things, hopes all things, and endures all things.

13:1-2. This chapter follows the end of chapter 12, where Paul said, "Earnestly desire the best gifts. Moreover, I show you a more excellent way" (1 Cor. 12:31). What are the best gifts? The "best" are those that we can use to serve others in love. Is it possible to speak in unlearned languages, prophesy, and have faith to move mountains—and still not love the people around us? Yes, Paul is using hypothetical language, but he points out that spiritual gifts are for the purpose of showing love to others. Even faith that can move mountains is futile if we do not love the people around us.

13:3: Even if I serve the poor by giving them food and shelter, but I do not really love them from my heart, there will be no reward for me in heaven. Review 1 Cor. 3:10-14.

Questions:

The words of 13:4-7 are often read at weddings. Discuss what these attributes of love mean to a newly married couple, and also what they mean in terms of our relationship with others in the church.

1 Corinthians 13:8-13   Love Never Fails

[8] Love never fails. But where there are prophecies, they will be done away with. Where there are various languages, they will cease. Where there is knowledge, it will be done away with. [9] For we know in part, and we prophesy in part; [10] but when that which is perfect has come, then that which is partial will be done away with. [11] When I was a child, I spoke as a child, I though as a child, I reasoned as a child. Now that I have become a man, I have put away childish things. [12] For now we see in a mirror, dimly, but then face to face. Now I know in part, but then I will know fully, even as I was also fully known. [13] But now these three remain: faith, hope, and love, but the greatest of these is love.

13:8. Love is the greatest fruit of the Spirit, and it has priority over all gifts and fruits of the Spirit. Love will endure even when other things are absent.

13:8-10. The gifts of the Spirit are temporary and will cease when this earth passes away and we see Christ face to face. Some theologians have argued that spiritual gifts ceased when the Bible was completed, because we no longer need spiritual gifts. They refer to v. 10, "When that which is perfect has come." However, that is not what Paul is teaching. Languages have not ceased, knowledge has not ceased, and prophetic utterances have not ceased. The Bible did not negate the need for spiritual gifts. If we look at the lists of gifts in Romans 12 and Ephesians 4, we see gifts such as pastor, teacher, serving, and giving. Some would argue that the serving gifts still remain, but the miraculous gifts ceased. This argument is based on observations but is nowhere taught in Scripture.

13:10-13. Paul speaks of spiritual maturity. In 1 Cor. 3:1-4, Paul told the people that they are still spiritual infants. Here again, he admonishes them to exercise their spiritual gifts with maturity and wisdom.

1 Corinthians Chapter 14

1 Corinthians 14:1-5   Build up the Church

[1] Follow after love and earnestly desire spiritual gifts, but especially that you may prophesy. [2] For he who speaks in another language speaks not to men, but to God, for no one understands him, but in the Spirit he speaks mysteries. [3] But he who prophesies speaks to men for their edification, exhortation, and comfort. [4] He who speaks in another language edifies himself, but he who prophesies edifies the church. [5] Now I wish that you all had the gift of speaking with other languages, but even more that you would prophesy, because he is greater who prophesies than he who speaks with other languages, unless he interprets, that the church may be built up.

14:1-5. Chapters 12-14 all have the same theme—how to behave in church. It is God's desire that every Christian have one or more spiritual gifts (1 Cor. 12:11), but when everyone tries to use their spiritual gift at the same time, it can result in chaos. Chapter 14 ends with the words, "Let all things be done decently and in order" (14:40).

14:1. "Earnestly desire spiritual gifts" is a command, and it implies that God will take our desires into account. God, however, is not obligated to give us what we want. Ultimately, God will provide us with what he wants for the church. Paul values prophecy because it helps to strengthen and build up the church. However, Paul is probably not elevating prophecy above all other gifts, but only in relationship to speaking in tongues (or languages). It was the speaking gifts—prophecy and languages—that were causing most of the problems in Corinth. People interrupted and talked over each other, taking unreasonable amounts of time so that others were not given time to exercise their gifts. We have them in every church!

14:2. There has been much debate whether the gift of languages (tongues) involves human languages, the language of angels (13:1), or just ecstatic gibberish. Paul brings some clarity to the issue here.

When someone speaks in a tongue, it is a language, but not a language that other humans can understand. This is different than the event in Acts 2 where each of those who heard understood the message in their own language. The miracle was in the hearing as much as in the speaking. There is no indication that such a phenomenon ever happened again after the Day of Pentecost. In Corinth, no one understood what was being said unless someone had the gift of interpretation. The person speaking in a language is speaking mysteries by the power of the Spirit (14:2).

14:3-4. The purpose of prophecy is to speak to people "for their edification, exhortation, and comfort" (v. 3). Thus, the primary purpose of prophecy in the New Testament Church is to convey a Spirit-inspired message to build up the church. Speaking in a language, however, builds up the individual speaking, but it does not help the hearers unless the message is interpreted.

14:5. The ultimate purpose of spiritual gifts is to serve the church. Therefore, Paul values those gifts that are more useful for the church. Speaking in a language is useful to the church if someone with the gift of interpretation is present, but if not, then the person should not speak in the church; instead, they should use their gift in their private prayer time (14:28).

Questions:

Many people have observed that we do not see the supernatural gifts of the Spirit in use today as much as they were in the Book of Acts and at Corinth. Why do you think that is?

Did Paul have a negative view of the gift of languages? Did he discourage the church from using this gift?

1 Corinthians 14:6-13   Orderliness in the Church

⁶But now, brothers, if I come to you speaking with other languages, what would I profit you unless I speak to you either by way of revelation, or of knowledge, or of prophesying, or of teaching? ⁷Even lifeless things that make a sound, whether pipe or harp, if they did not give a distinction in the sounds, how would it be known what is piped or harped? ⁸For if the trumpet gave an uncertain sound, who would prepare himself for war? ⁹So also you, unless you speak words easy to understand, how would it be known what you are speaking; you would be speaking into the air. ¹⁰There are, it may be, so many kinds of languages in the world, and none of them is without meaning. ¹¹If then I do not know the meaning of the language, I would be to him who speaks a foreigner, and he who speaks would be a foreigner to me. ¹²So you also, since you are zealous for spiritual gifts, seek that you may excel in the building up of the church. ¹³Therefore, let him who speaks in another language pray that he may interpret.

14:6-11. Paul continues the theme that speaking in unknown languages is of no benefit to the hearers in the church unless the message is interpreted. However, prophecy in a known language is of great benefit.

14:12-13. It's great to desire spiritual gifts, but especially to seek those that will help the entire church. You can also pray for certain gifts. If you already have the gift of languages, pray that you may also have the gift of interpretation.

1 Corinthians 14:14-19   Praying with the Spirit

¹⁴ For if I pray in another language, my spirit prays, but I do not understand with my mind what I am saying. ¹⁵ What should I do? I will pray with the spirit, and I will pray with my mind also. I will sing with the spirit, and I will sing with my mind also. ¹⁶ Otherwise, if you bless with the spirit, how will he who fills the place of the unlearned say the "Amen" at your giving of thanks, seeing he does not know what you say? ¹⁷ For you most certainly give thanks well, but the other person is not built up. ¹⁸ I thank my God that I speak with other languages more than all of you. ¹⁹ However, in the church, I would rather speak five words with my mind that I might instruct others also, than ten thousand words in another language.

14:14-15. Praying in a spiritual language comes from the Holy Spirit as he resides in the human spirit. Such prayer is not formulated in the human mind and is not understood by the mind.

Paul not only prayed in languages, but he also sang in languages.

14:16-19. Paul says that he would rather speak five words in a language that people can understand than speak ten thousand words in an unknown language.

Questions:

What do you think of Paul's statement that he speaks in languages more than all of you?

What are your thoughts about this gift?

1 Corinthians 14:21-25   What Will People Think?

²¹ It is written in the Law, "By men of strange languages and by the lips of strangers I will speak to this people, and even then they will not listen to me, says the Lord." ²² Therefore, unknown languages are for a sign, not to those who believe, but to the unbelieving; but prophesying is for a sign, not to the unbelieving, but to those who believe. ²³ If therefore the whole church is assembled together and all speak with other languages, and unlearned or unbelieving people come in, will they not say that you are crazy? ²⁴ But if all prophesy, and someone unbelieving or unlearned comes in, he is reproved by all, and he is judged by all. ²⁵ And thus the secrets of his heart are revealed. So he will fall down on his face and worship God, declaring that God is among you indeed.

14:20-25. Verses 22 through 25 present a riddle. Verse 22 states that unknown languages are a sign to unbelievers, but verse 23 says that unbelievers will reject the sign. The answer to the riddle lies in the quotation from verse 21, where Paul quotes from Isaiah 28:11-12. In the Isaiah quotation, Israel will understand that they are under divine judgment when they hear the strange language of foreigners, but still they do not repent. Thus, the sign to unbelievers is not a sign that brings them to Christ the way that prophecy does.[5]

Setting aside the complications, Paul's previous assertions still hold true: prophecy is more valuable in the public worship service than speaking in unknown languages.

---

[5] For more on this complicated interpretation, see Mark Taylor, *1 Corinthians* (Nashville: Broadman and Holman, 2014), 341; Gordon Fee, *The First Epistle to the Corinthians*, 680-683; Thomas R. Schreiner, 1 *Corinthians: An Introduction and Commentary*, Tyndale New Testament Commentaries (Downers Grove: InterVarsity Press, 2018), 378-380.

1 Corinthians 14:26-33   Using Your Gifts in Harmony

> [26] What is it then, brothers? When you come together, each one of you has a psalm, has a teaching, has a revelation, has another language, or has an interpretation. Let all things be done to build each other up. [27] If any man speaks in another language, let there be two, or at the most three, and in turn, and let one interpret. [28] But if there is no interpreter, let him keep silent in the assembly, and let him speak to himself and to God. [29] Let two or three of the prophets speak, and let the others discern. [30] But if a revelation is made to another sitting by, let the first keep silent. [31] For you all can prophesy one by one, that all may learn and all may be exhorted. [32] The spirits of the prophets are subject to the prophets, [33] for God is not a God of confusion but of peace, as in all the churches of the saints.

14:26-31. Paul expected the worship experience to be vibrant and participatory. It probably lasted several hours, and many people came expecting to use their spiritual gift. Those in charge are required to set limits. No more than two, or at the most three, could speak in unknown languages, and then only if there was an interpreter present. Likewise, with the prophets—two or three could speak, and the spiritual leaders should listen and discern if the prophetic message is truly from God.

14:31. "The spirits of the prophets are subject to the prophets." This implies that people should not use the excuse—"I have to speak because I am under the inspiration of the Spirit." Even though you feel the urge to use your spiritual gift, it is still under your control. Whether the gift is speaking in a language or prophesying, the Spirit will not force the person to speak, and the speaker must exercise self-discipline and speak only when it is appropriate. The elders in charge may ask someone to stop talking so that someone else may have the opportunity to share their gift.

Question: The presence of spiritual gifts can cause confusion and may be hard to manage. Is it still worth it? Should churches encourage people to seek spiritual gifts?

1 Corinthians 14:34-35   Final Words about Gifts

[34] Women should remain silent in the churches. They are not allowed to speak, but must be in submission, as the law says. [35] If they want to inquire about something, they should ask their own husbands at home, for it is disgraceful for a woman to speak in the church. NIV.

14:34-35. Women must remain silent in the churches. There are several views on how this should be interpreted.

One view: At all times and in all places, women must remain absolutely silent in church. The problem with this interpretation is that Paul acknowledged that women pray and prophesy in church (1 Cor. 11:1-10). Also, in the instructions on spiritual gifts (Chapters 12-14), Paul does not distinguish between men and women, and it would seem that he anticipated that both would use their gifts in the church.

Another view: The church at Corinth had specific problems that Paul was trying to address, and the solution was geared to the problem. We have already seen that Paul was concerned that the Christians at Corinth should not do anything that would bring scandal upon the church. For a woman to go out in public with her hair uncovered would be scandalous at that time (1 Cor. 11:1-16). Also, when Paul says that if a woman has any questions, she should ask her husband at home, he may be defining the problem he is trying to solve.

In Paul's letters to Timothy, he laid out additional rules for women. Women are not allowed to teach or hold authority over a man (1 Tim. 2:11-15). The Corinthian rules and Paul's instructions to Timothy should be considered alongside each other. There is no indication that the instructions to Timothy were based on the problems of a particular church, such as the one at Corinth. Timothy was in Ephesus at the time, but apparently Paul intended the same rules to apply to all churches.

If we want to remain true to Scripture, we must find a solution that honors God's word while also recognizing that in Paul's time, women did exercise spiritual gifts in the church. In 11:5-6 Paul says that it is a shame for a woman to pray or prophesy with her head uncovered. This implies that she is praying and prophesying in the worship service; if she were doing it at home with her husband, her hair would not be an issue. Hair becomes an issue based on the cultural standards of the day. Paul is willing to give up all of his rights in order to avoid bringing shame on the church, and he expects all believers to do the same. He wanted the slaves of his day to put up with their enslavement rather than put up a fight that would break the unity of the church. But if the cultural conditions changed, and slaves could gain their freedom, he expected them to do so.

1 Corinthians 14:36-38

[36] Or did the word of God originate with you? Or are you the only people it has reached? [37] If anyone thinks they are a prophet or otherwise gifted by the Spirit, let them acknowledge that what I am writing to you is the Lord's command. [38] But if anyone ignores this, they will themselves be ignored.

[39] Therefore, my brothers and sisters, be eager to prophesy, and do not forbid speaking in tongues. [40] But everything should be done in a fitting and orderly way. NIV

14:36-38. Paul anticipates that some in Corinth will refute his apostolic authority and the validity of his instructions to them. With some degree of sarcasm, he asks, "Did the word of God originate with you?" If you truly have the Spirit, as you claim, you must recognize that my words are not really my own, but they are the commands of God.

14:39. "Be eager to prophesy" ... as Paul wrote before, "eagerly desire the best gifts", "especially that you may prophesy" (12:31; 14:1); and, do not forbid speaking in unknown languages (tongues). By this last phrase, Paul wants to make clear that he is not forbidding speaking in other languages, but only that it be done in an orderly way that benefits the church.

1 Corinthians Chapter 15

1 Corinthians 15:1-11   Defense of Paul's Apostleship

¹ Now I declare to you, brothers, the gospel which I preached to you, which also you received, in which you also stand, ² by which also you are saved, if you hold firmly the word which I preached to you—unless you believed in vain.

³ For I delivered to you first of all that which I also received: that Christ died for our sins according to the Scriptures, ⁴ that he was buried, that he was raised on the third day according to the Scriptures, ⁵ and that he appeared to Cephas, then to the twelve. ⁶ Then he appeared to over five hundred brothers at once, most of whom remain until now, but some have also fallen asleep. ⁷ Then he appeared to James, then to all the apostles, ⁸ and last of all, as to the child born at the wrong time, he appeared to me also. ⁹ For I am the least of the apostles, who is not worthy to be called an apostle, because I persecuted the church of God. ¹⁰ But by the grace of God I am what I am. His grace which was given to me was not futile, but I worked more than all of them; yet not I, but the grace of God which was with me. ¹¹ Whether then it is I or they, so we preach, and so you believed.

15:1-2. In his closing words of what has become chapter 14, Paul asserts that he is truly an apostle and his words are the commandments of God. He now continues that defense. As the founder of the church at Corinth, many of the converts there came to know Christ because of Paul's preaching, and they will be saved if they hold firm to the word that he preached. He is encouraging them not to depart from the true gospel and follow after false teachers.

15:3-7. Paul preached to them how that Jesus died and rose again, and was then seen alive by many witnesses, including the eleven apostles. Last of all (after the ones previously mentioned), Jesus also appeared to Paul. Some take this "last of all" (v. 7) to mean that no one else after him could ever become an apostle, but the text does not say that. Seeing the risen Christ was a requirement for the twelve (Acts 1:21-22), but there were other apostles who did not meet these requirements. Paul did not meet all of the requirements set out for the twelve (he did not accompany Jesus during his earthly ministry), and Barnabas was an apostle, and he did not see Christ (Acts 14:14).

15:6. Paul is the only source who tells us that over 500 people witnessed Christ alive after the resurrection.

15:9-10. "For I am the least of the apostles, who is not worthy to be called an apostle, because I persecuted the church of God." Although Paul feels he needs to defend his apostleship in the midst of his critics, he is still humbled by the fact that God called him despite his murderous past. "But by the grace of God, I am what I am."

15:11. "Whether then it is I or they, so we preach, and so you believed." Paul is simply thankful that the people of Corinth have come to know Christ, regardless of whose preaching led them to Christ. Paul does not need to take credit; it is all for God's glory.

1 Corinthians 15:12-19

[12] Now if Christ is preached, that he has been raised from the dead, how do some among you say that there is no resurrection of the dead? [13] But if there is no resurrection of the dead, neither has Christ been raised. [14] If Christ has not been raised, then our preaching is in vain and your faith also is in vain. [15] Yes, we are also found false witnesses of God, because we testified about God that he raised up Christ, whom he did not raise up if it is true that the dead are not raised. [16] For if the dead are not raised, neither has Christ been raised. [17] If Christ has not been raised, your faith is vain; you are still in your sins. [18] Then they also who are fallen asleep in Christ have perished. [19] If we have only hoped in Christ in this life, we are of all men most pitiful

15:12. There were some Christians in Corinth who denied that Jesus actually rose from the dead. This teaching may have come from the

Sadducees, who denied the resurrection (Matt. 22:23); or it may have been a form of Gnosticism, which was prevalent in the first and second centuries. Some Gnostics also embraced Docetism, which is a denial that Jesus actually had a physical body. Although the evidence is inconclusive, some historians believe that the Gnostics also baptized for the dead;[6] if that is the case, the same Gnostics who denied the resurrection also vicariously baptized for the dead (15:29).

15:14-19. If Christ is not raised from the dead, then there is no hope of salvation for us Christians. "If Christ has not been raised, your faith is vain; you are still in your sins" (v. 17).

Paul included belief in the resurrection of Jesus as a core belief necessary for salvation (Rom. 10:9-10)

The Christian's hope is that Christ died to pay the penalty for our sins, and his resurrection is proof of his victory over sin, death, and the grave.

Questions:

In many parts of the world today, people are persecuted and often die for their faith in Christ. Why is it important for them to know that there is life after death?

All of the early apostles were persecuted for their faith. What motivated them to accept persecution, including death, if they did not believe that they would be resurrected into eternity?

---

[6] Mark Taylor, *1 Corinthians*, 393. The Church of Latter-Day Saints (Mormon) also baptizes for the dead.

1 Corinthians 15:20-26   The Resurrection Continued

> [20] But now Christ has been raised from the dead. He became the first fruit of those who are asleep. [21] For since death came by man, the resurrection of the dead also came by man. [22] For as in Adam all die, so also in Christ all will be made alive. [23] But each in his own order: Christ the first fruits, then those who are Christ's at his coming. [24] Then the end comes, when he will deliver up the Kingdom to God the Father, when he will have abolished all rule and all authority and power. [25] For he must reign until he has put all his enemies under his feet. [26] The last enemy that will be abolished is death.

15:20-23. V. 22 is complicated on the surface. We understand that in Adam all humans inherited the sin nature and are separated from God in a spiritual sense. It is not clear, however, how all are made alive in Christ if the term "all" means the same thing in both cases. Some interpret "all will be made alive" to be limited to all who are in Christ will be made alive.[7] This seems to be the consensus interpretation.

15:24-26. These verses point to an event at the end of the millennial kingdom. If the rapture of the church is pretribulation, then there is a gap between verses 23 and 24, such that they refer to separate events. The plain reading of the text seems to favor one event that occurs at the end of the millennial kingdom.

---

[7] Gordon Fee, *The First Epistle to the Corinthians*, 750; Mark Taylor, *1 Corinthians*, 392; Thomas R. Schreiner, *1 Corinthians*, 405.

1 Corinthians 15:35-44   The Resurrection Body

[35] But someone will say, "How are the dead raised?" and, "With what kind of body do they come?" [36] You foolish one, that which you yourself sow is not made alive unless it dies. [37] That which you sow, you do not sow the body that will be, but a bare grain, maybe of wheat, or of some other kind. [38] But God gives it a body even as it pleased him, and to each seed a body of its own. [39] All flesh is not the same flesh, but there is one flesh of men, another flesh of animals, another of fish, and another of birds. [40] There are also celestial bodies and terrestrial bodies; but the glory of the celestial differs from that of the terrestrial. [41] There is one glory of the sun, another glory of the moon, and another glory of the stars; for one star differs from another star in glory.

[42] So also is the resurrection of the dead. The body is sown perishable; it is raised imperishable. [43] It is sown in dishonor; it is raised in glory. It is sown in weakness; it is raised in power. [44] It is sown a natural body; it is raised a spiritual body. There is a natural body and there is also a spiritual body.

15:34-44. The resurrected body is not a flesh and blood body like the earthly body. Scripture does not tell us what the substance of the heavenly body is because it is not made of earthly material. God formed man from the dust of the earth (Gen. 2:7).

15:43. The earthly body is weak; the resurrected body is strong. This strength is no doubt physical as well as spiritual. The angels have supernatural strength. The key to their strength is tied to the principle that the spiritual world has authority over the physical world.

1 Corinthians 15:51-58   **Resurrection and Rapture**

[51] Behold, I tell you a mystery. We will not all sleep, but we will all be changed, [52] in a moment, in the twinkling of an eye, at the last trumpet. For the trumpet will sound and the dead will be raised incorruptible, and we will be changed. [53] For this perishable body must become imperishable, and this mortal must put on immortality. [54] But when this perishable body will have become imperishable, and this mortal will have put on immortality, then what is written will happen: "Death is swallowed up in victory."

[55] "Death, where is your sting?
  Hades, where is your victory?"

[56] The sting of death is sin, and the power of sin is the law. [57] But thanks be to God, who gives us the victory through our Lord Jesus Christ. [58] Therefore, my beloved brothers, be steadfast, immovable, always abounding in the Lord's work, because you know that your labor is not in vain in the Lord.

15:51-54. This passage parallels Paul's teaching on the rapture of the church in 1 Thess. 413:18. He has prepared the way in vs 20-50 in teaching about the nature of the resurrected body, but now in vs 51-52 he mentions a specific event in which "we will all be changed."

Paul has discussed the resurrection throughout chapter 15, and it is apparent that he is referring to the same event.

1 Corinthians Chapter 16

1 Corinthians 16:1-9   Closing Comments and Instruction

[1] Now concerning the collection for the saints: as I told the churches of Galatia, you do likewise. [2] On the first day of every week, let each one of you give according to his income, that no collections are made when I come. [3] When I arrive, I will send whoever you approve with letters to carry your gracious gift to Jerusalem. [4] If it is appropriate for me to go also, they will go with me.

[5] I will come to you when I have passed through Macedonia, for I am passing through Macedonia. [6] But with you it may be that I will stay with you, or even winter with you, that you may send me on my journey wherever I go. [7] For I do not wish to see you now in passing, but I hope to stay a while with you, if the Lord permits. [8] But I will stay at Ephesus until Pentecost, [9] for a great and effective door has opened to me, and there are many

---

16:1-2. Jerusalem was experiencing a famine at the time of this writing, and Paul had asked the churches to collect money for a benevolence gift to help the Christians in Jerusalem. Paul never mentions tithing in his letters. New Testament giving is always voluntary as the Spirit directs. On this same matter, Paul wrote to the church at Corinth:

> Remember this: he who sows sparingly will also reap sparingly. He who sows bountifully will also reap bountifully. Let each man give according as he has determined in his heart, not grudgingly or under compulsion, for God loves a cheerful giver.   2 Cor. 9:6-7

1 Corinthians 16:10-24   Closing Comments and Instruction

[10] Now if Timothy comes, see that he is with you without fear, for he does the work of the Lord, as I also do. [11] Therefore let no one despise him. But set him forward on his journey in peace, that he may come to me; for I expect him with the brothers.

[12] Now concerning Apollos the brother, I strongly urged him to come to you with the brothers, but it was not at all his desire to come now; but he will come when he has an opportunity.

[13] Watch! Stand firm in the faith! Be courageous! Be strong! [14] Let all that you do be done in love.

[15] Now I beg you, brothers, you know that the house of Stephanas was the first fruit of Achaia, and that they have set themselves to serve the saints— [16] that you also submit to them, and to everyone who helps in the work and labors. [17] I rejoice at the coming of Stephanas, Fortunatus, and Achaicus; for that which was lacking on your part, they supplied. [18] For they refreshed my spirit and yours. Therefore, acknowledge those who are like that.

[19] The churches of Asia greet you. Aquila and Priscilla greet you warmly in the Lord, together with the church that is in their house. [20] All the brothers greet you. Greet one another with a holy kiss.

[21] This greeting is by me, Paul, with my own hand. [22] If anyone does not love the Lord Jesus Christ, let him be cursed. Come, Lord! [23] The grace of the Lord Jesus Christ be with you. [24] My love to all of you in Christ Jesus. Amen.

16:12. Concerning Apollos… In chapter 1, where Paul chides the church for their divisions, some of the people claimed to be followers of Apollos. Paul does not hold this against Apollos personally, and he sees Apollos as his fellow laborer in Christ. Paul urged Apollos to travel to Corinth, but Apollos was unwilling to go at the present time.

The fact that Paul asked him to go to Corinth is a further indication that Paul does not see Apollos as a threat or as a cause of the divisions.

16:13-14. Paul considers himself a father to the people in Corinth. It is only natural that he gives them some fatherly encouragement. "Watch! Stand firm in the faith! Be courageous! Be strong! Let all that you do be done in love."

16:19. Aquila and Priscilla lived in Corinth when Paul was there planting the church (Acts 18). At the time of this writing, they are in Ephesus along with Timothy (2 Tim. 4:19). Wherever they traveled, they hosted a church in their home.

16:20. Greet one another with a holy kiss. It is obvious that this, although stated as a command, is actually a request based on local customs. This is another indicator that some of Paul's language is based on cultural customs.

Questions:

Would the holy kiss be appropriate for today? Have you noticed cultural differences in other parts of the world? For example, people in Europe greet each other with a kiss on the cheek more so than in America.

What are your thoughts about Paul's comments in v. 22?

Bibliography

Fee, Gordon. *The First Epistle to the Corinthians*, The New International Commentary on the New Testament. Grand Rapids: Eerdmans, 1987.

Keener, Craig. *1-2 Corinthians*. Cambridge: Cambridge Univ. Press, 2005.

Morris, Leon. *1 Corinthians*. Grand Rapids, Inter-Varsity Press, 1983.

Osborn, Grant, ed. *1 and 2 Corinthians, Life Application Commentary*. Carol Stream: Tyndale House, 1999.

Schreiner, Thomas R. 1 *Corinthians: An Introduction and Commentary*, Tyndale New Testament Commentaries. Downers Grove: InterVarsity Press, 2018.

Taylor, Mark. *1 Corinthians*. Nashville: Broadman and Holman, 2014.

www.ingramcontent.com/pod-product-compliance
Lightning Source LLC
Chambersburg PA
CBHW071929020426
42331CB00010B/2787